Steps to European unity

**Community progress
to date:
a chronology**

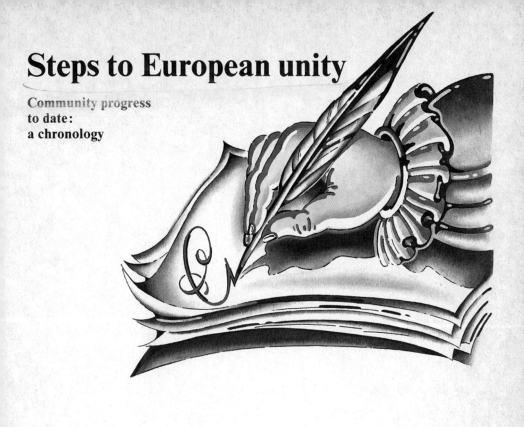

This publication also appears in the following languages:

DA   ISBN 92-825-1550-8
DE   ISBN 92-825-1551-6
FR   ISBN 92-825-1553-2
IT   ISBN 92-825-1554-0
NL   ISBN 92-825-1555-9

Cataloguing data can be found at the end of this publication

Reproduction authorized in whole or in part, provided the source is acknowledged.

Printed in the FR of Germany 1980

ISBN 92-825-1552-4   Catalogue number: CB-28-79-641-EN-C

Contents

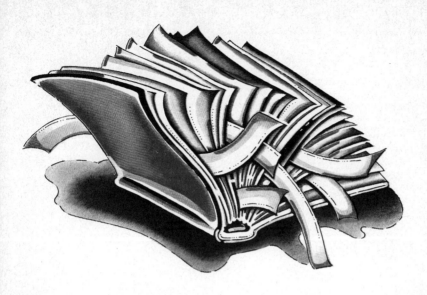

Introduction

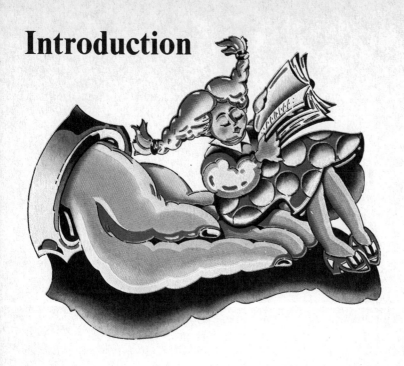

Every day the European Community organizes meetings of parliamentarians, ambassadors, industrialists, workers, managers, ministers, consumers, people from all walks of life, working for a common response to problems that for a long time now have transcended national frontiers.

It is not an easy task.

Unlike all the earlier efforts to unite Europe by force, the Community's objective is unity by mutual consent, and it is striving towards a union based on a freely-accepted body of law. By the very nature of things progress is slow and laborious and sometimes made only reluctantly, for it is never easy for any government to give up its powers and prerogatives, and no administration is happy to abandon its traditions.

But the young of today – those with whom the future of Europe lies – are losing hope and interest. The Community's hesitations and failures, which regularly make the newspaper headlines, are not, to the minds of young people, what a united Europe is all about.

It is the good fortune of young people today that they do not harbour the hatred and prejudice born of the progression of wars that constitutes our continent's history. What counts in their eyes is working together to master the many problems facing the modern world.

What is important to them is the role that their European continent, their country and their region will have to play in a world where everything is changing, and changing fast. What interests them is the evolution of a society that they, like every generation of young people before them, wish to make more generous and more human.

What young people often fail to realize is that progress actually has been made, that Europe really has begun advancing towards integration and that there has been a definite change in attitudes of mind.

The aim of this modest booklet is to outline and explain the facts and trends of an all too complex process.

We have not written a textbook on the history of the European Community, nor even a full chronology, for that would have filled a far larger volume. All we have set out to do is describe the main stages in the construction of the European Community, highlighting the key events at each stage of its history.

We begin in 1945 with a Europe licking its wounds as so often before, trying to pick up the pieces after the Second World War; we end in 1979 with the emergence of an embryonic European currency. No attempt will be made to conceal the many serious setbacks that have hampered progress along the road to unity.

First hopes,
first failures
1950 – 1954

1945 – 1950   The victory of the allied powers over Nazi Germany, which brings the Second World War in Europe to an end, once again leaves Europe licking its wounds, a continent in ruins, impoverished and enfeebled, brimming with hatred.

The only real victors in this European civil war are the United States and the Soviet Union. The two great powers, each profoundly convinced of the inherent superiority of its own ideology, dominate the world and its immediate future.

At the same time there are countries in Africa and Asia, many of which have been involved in the war, that are waking up and demanding independence from their weakened colonial masters in Europe.

These are the circumstances in which farsighted politicians, just like certain resistance movements in the two wars, awake to their duty.

19 – 9 – 1946   On 19 September 1946 Winston Churchill, who, as British Prime Minister, played such an eminent role in the struggle against Nazism, makes his now famous speech at Zurich calling for the establishment of a United States of Europe. This has a truly sensational impact, for here is the response both to the overwhelming desire for peace among the peoples of Europe while at the same time, in a continent where poverty, revenge and hatred still reign supreme, the banner of hope and generosity is raised, the first real step towards reconciliation is taken.

9 – 5 – 1950   This is the date on which the European Communities as we know them celebrate their 'birthday'. The French Minister of Foreign Affairs, Robert Schuman, in a speech on behalf of the French Government, proposes pooling the production and consumption of coal and steel and setting up a European organization for the purpose, bringing France and the Federal Republic of Germany together. The organization would

be open to all the countries in Europe and would be directed by an European institution, to be called the High Authority. But whatever the economic importance of this community, its political importance is even greater, for its authors are laying the foundation stone of a European federation.

For the first time in their history, national governments are asked to delegate part of their sovereignty, albeit in limited, clearly-defined matters, to a High Authority consisting of persons chosen by them but acting independently and collectively enjoying powers to take decisions in the common interest of the Member States.

This is the really novel element in the first European Community – the European Coal and Steel Community (ECSC).

As well as the High Authority, the ECSC is given a Council of Ministers, a Court of Justice and a Parliamentary Assembly.

In this new institutional structure, decisions are taken by the High Authority and by the Council. The latter consists of Ministers representing the governments of the Member States. The Court of Justice settles disputes between the High Authority and the governments and citizens of the Member States. The Assembly gives opinions but does not have legislative powers.

The whole idea is bold and revolutionary for its day and its success owes much to the conviction with which Jean Monnet, at that time France's Commissaire au Plan (National Plan Commissioner), advanced the scheme, and the political courage and determination shown by Robert Schuman in carrying the idea through.

Together, Jean Monnet, the planner, the creative genius who sought to build the future out of the ruins of the past, and Robert Schuman, whose home was Lorraine in France and who had experienced at first hand the effects of enmity and warfare between France and Germany, are able to bring about this fundamental step towards a united Europe.

The geopolitical context helps too. From the East the spectre of Soviet Communism looms large and there is a crying need for the Western nations to work out where they stand on the world's political stage.

Against this background, the Federal Republic of Germany, Italy, Belgium, the Netherlands and the Grand Duchy of Luxembourg, are quick to endorse the plan.

18 – 4 – 1951   The first Community is set up by a Treaty signed in Paris on 18 April 1951 (Paris Treaty establishing the European Coal and Steel Community), and swiftly ratified by the parliaments of the Six Member States in the winter and spring of 1952.

1951

The United Kingdom, however, declines the invitation to join a Community whose rules seem rather too binding for its taste.

27 – 5 – 1952 The inherent dynamism of the new-born Europe prompts plans for two new communities – the European Defence Community (EDC), based on a treaty signed by the Six on 27 May 1952, and a European Political Community.

The EDC is inspired by the political and, more especially, the military situation of the time. The tensions created by the developing cold war and the partition of Germany and Berlin lead to a deterioration in East West relations and the EDC is conceived as a means of bolstering the Atlantic Alliance. The aim is to integrate the armed forces of Western Europe.

But an integrated European army is unthinkable without a common European foreign policy, and so the foreign ministers of the Six call on the ECSC Parliamentary Assembly to prepare a plan for a political Community.

9 – 3 – 1953 A report submitted to the six governments states that the new community should enjoy powers in the fields of foreign affairs, defence, economic and social integration and protection of human rights. It is also proposed that a new federal type of organization be set up to absorb the ECSC and the EDC within two years. Throughout Europe, and even in the very Assembly that devised it, keen controversy surrounds the plan.

30 – 8 – 1954 Failure comes in the middle of the summer. As soon as the French Parliament begins debating ratification of the EDC Treaty, it becomes clear that there will not be a majority in favour. On 30 August 1954, before the Treaty is even put to the vote in Italy, the French National Assembly rejects the plan outright.

Reactions to the failure vary. Many are saddened by the defeat of this attempt to create a new Europe in a single, powerful burst of enthusiasm. Others argue that Europe is perhaps trying to integrate too fast and that a community created solely in response to the pressure of outside events will be a fragile community indeed.

Birth of the
Common Market
1955 – 1962

1/2 – 6 – 1955   Within a few months the governments of Europe have learnt the lessons of the failure of the EDC. But most of them are unshaken in their desire to press ahead with the unification of Europe.

Meeting at Messina at the beginning of June 1955, the Foreign Ministers of the Six announce that they intend to continue the attempt to establish a united Europe so as to preserve Europe's role in the world, restore its influence and prestige, and steadily increase the standard of living of its people.

But, reacting cautiously to the failure of the EDC, they decide to begin by developing European union on the economic front. An intergovernmental committee, chaired by Paul-Henri Spaak, Belgian statesman and ardent supporter of the European cause, is set up to report on the prospects for general economic union and for union in the field of nuclear energy.

29 – 5 – 1956   Europe is on the move again. On 29 May 1956, Foreign Ministers, meeting in Venice, approve the Spaak Report and decide to begin intergovernmental negotiations in which the Six and other countries in Europe are invited to take part.

Since these negotiations are to lead to the establishment of new communities and hence of new common policies, the United Kingdom decides not to take part; in October 1956 it announces its preference for a free-trade area.

13 – 2 – 1957   In February 1957 the Council of the Organization for European Economic Cooperation (OEEC) begins negotiations for the establishment of a free-trade area.

While continuing their own efforts to integrate, the Six express willingness to take part in the OEEC negotiations.

25 – 3 – 1957   At the same time, then, there are two separate series of negotiations; one culminates in the Treaties of Rome signed by the Six on 25 March 1957 and the other in the formation of the European Free Trade Association (EFTA) on 3 May 1960. EFTA consists of Austria, Denmark, Norway, Portugal, Sweden, Switzerland and the United Kingdom.

The Rome Treaties establishing the European Economic Community (EEC) and the European Atomic Energy Community (Euratom), together with the Paris Treaty establishing the European Coal and Steel Community (ECSC), form the constitution of the European Community.

Ratified within a few months by the parliaments of all the signatory States, the Rome Treaties receive far greater majorities than the Paris Treaty – a symptom of growing enthusiasm for European integration. The European treaties all have the same objectives – economic expansion and higher standards of living, accompanied by political union of the peoples of Europe.

The EEC Treaty's immediate objectives are the establishment of a customs union with free movement of goods between Member States, the dismantling of quotas and barriers to trade of all kinds, and the free movement of persons, services and capital.

But going beyond this, the Treaty provides for a number of common policies on matters such as agriculture, transport and competition; the harmonization of legislation; a social policy; an external trade policy and so on.

Moreover, the preamble and the general clauses of the EEC Treaty call for the implementation of common policies and rules in virtually all areas of economic and social life. A special article empowers the Community institutions to set up any policies – even if not specifically provided for by the Treaty – that may be necessary to attain the general objectives set out in the Treaty. It is under this article that the Community gradually develops policies to deal with the great industrial problems of the day, a regional policy (not provided for in the Treaty) and a social policy, a policy on the environment, a policy on consumer protection and proposals for a passport union, to name but a few.

In its endeavours to attain the four great freedoms (free movement of persons, of goods, of services and of capital), the Community begins tackling the problem of right of establishment, achieves free movement for all workers, sets about harmonizing national legislation and gradually creates a single market. But much still remains to be done.

The Community, originally dependent upon contributions from the Member States for its financial resources, eventually embarks on a budgetary policy providing it with substantial resources of its own.

But the Treaty is virtually silent on matters of general economic and monetary policy since at the time it was drafted, economic growth and convergence were largely taken for granted.

Foreign policy, on the other hand, remains the prerogative of the Member States themselves. *Vis-à-vis* non-member countries, the Community's powers are confined to establishing a common commercial policy. In pursuit of this goal, however, a wide variety of agreements have been concluded between the Community and virtually the whole of the rest of the world.

Right from the start the Treaty imposes on the Community specific duties in relation to the former colonies of the Member States. Step by step, a general policy has been worked out on relations with all the developing countries.

The EAEC Treaty (generally referred to as the Euratom Treaty) provides for the joint development of nuclear energy for peaceful purposes. Euratom is the result of a burst of enthusiasm for nuclear power which is seen at the time as the answer to Europe's energy supply problems. But Euratom quickly runs into difficulties as the Member States fail to agree on the action to be taken to develop in common this revolutionary energy source.

1 – 1 – 1958   The EEC and Euratom Treaties enter into force on 1 January 1958. By the spring, the institutions of the two new Communities – the Commissions and the Councils consisting of ministers from the Member States – have been set up and are ready to get down to business. The Parliamentary Assembly and the Court of Justice are common to all three Communities (ECSC, EEC and Euratom).

The EEC Commission, which has the broadest range of functions, has nine members; its President is Walter Hallstein, one of the leading EEC Treaty negotiators and an outstanding figure in the process of building Europe.

19 – 3 – 1958   The Assembly elects Robert Schuman to be its President. This great pioneer of European unity can thus go on working for the achievement of his grand design.

1 – 1 – 1959   During the first few years after the signing of the EEC Treaty, substantial achievements are chalked up. The first cut in customs duties in trade between the Member States is made on 1 January 1959. All these customs duties are to be abolished gradually according to a timetable set out in the EEC Treaty, though not for agricultural produce. In trade with the rest of the world, a common external customs tariff is gradually set up at the same time.

8 – 6 – 1959   The progress that the Community has made and the hopes that it inspires begin to seem attractive to a number of non-member countries. On 8 June 1959 Greece applies to become an associated State with the European Economic Commu-

31 – 7 – 1959   nity, and six weeks later, on 31 July 1959, Turkey follows suit.

20 – 9 – 1960   The Treaty gives the European Coal and Steel Community extensive powers and financial resources to deal with problems arising in the coal and steel sectors – to provide assistance, for example, to workers made redundant.

Since the EEC Treaty has not clearly provided for a similar kind of social policy, the Council of the Six adopts the first regulation on the European Social Fund in 1960. The Fund is to provide assistance to workers and firms so that they can adapt to rapidly changing economic circumstances.

10/11 – 2 – 1961 The economic progress made by the Community and the continuing desire for closer cooperation in matters which are not specifically economic bring political cooperation back into the limelight.

At a Summit Conference of Heads of State or of Government of the Member States in February 1961, it is agreed that a political union should be set up between the Six.

A few months later on 18 July 1961, the leaders of the Six agree to hold regular meetings for general political consultation.

On 2 November 1961 a plan for political union worked out by a committee chaired by French politician, Christian Fouchet, is published. But neither this plan nor the next one (the second Fouchet plan) is approved by the Six. They fail because the larger and the smaller Community countries cannot agree on the way political cooperation should work. The large Community countries are reluctant to hand over the direction of foreign affairs to the Community's less flexible institutional machinery. The smaller Benelux countries on the other hand, fearing the prospect of a directory of the larger countries, prefer the more egalitarian decision-making procedures of the Community which they regard as better geared to produce solutions reflecting everybody's interests.

31 – 7 – 1961
9 – 8 – 1961
10 – 8 – 1961
In July and August 1961 Ireland, Denmark and the United Kingdom submit applications for membership of the European Communities.

Europe is on the move, and changing its dimension. Three countries which originally felt unable to join in the venture have finally concluded that they, too, should work for integration.

The applications from these three countries have a major impact on public opinion worldwide.

Some months later, on 30 April 1962, Norway tables its application for Community membership.

1 – 9 – 1961
The first regulation on free movement of workers from Member States within the Community comes into force. It opens up the frontiers to job seekers from all the Member States and protects them by giving them the same rights and obligations as nationals of whatever country they go to.

6/7 – 12 – 1961 On 6 and 7 December 1961 the Six and a large number of African countries meet in conference in Brussels.

In 1957 the Treaty of Rome had taken into account the special relations between certain Member States and their colonies. At the time France still had a number of territories in Africa, Belgium was responsible for the Congo and administered Rwanda and Burundi as trustee for the United Nations, while Italy administered Somalia as trustee.

To preserve the interests of these territories and of the Member States concerned, the Treaty provided for a commercial association with the African territories.

Policy in relation to these countries developed rapidly. Most of the African countries became independent early in the 1960s.

The Brussels conference of December 1961 is the first step in the Community's association with the developing countries.

January 1962 Agricultural policy has been at the centre of Community concern for a long time now. It is provided for by the Treaty and its broad lines were worked out at the Stresa conference in July 1958. Right from the beginning is was clearly impossible, for economic, human and political reasons, to establish free movement of farm produce without suitable safeguard measures, for there were specific bodies of regulations governing farming in all the Member States.

Ever since the EEC Treaty came into force, the elaboration of a common agricultural policy was a cornerstone in European integration, on a par with the establishment of a customs union.

The common agricultural policy is born in January 1962 following lengthy and often bitter negotiations and the longest negotiating marathon in the Community's history.

It is based on the following principles: establishment of a single market and consequently of common prices for most agricultural products; the assurance that those working in agriculture will enjoy a standard of living comparable to that enjoyed by workers in other sectors; preference for Community produce; financial solidarity through a European Agricultural Guidance and Guarantee Fund (EAGGF).

14 – 1 – 1962   By and large, progress so far has been fairly good. Indeed the European Economic Community has advanced so far that, with retroactive effect from 1 January 1962, the Council decrees the transition to the second stage of integration prescribed by the EEC Treaty.

1962

9 – 2 – 1962   The Spanish Government asks to begin negotiations for Community association. Portugal follows three months later on 18 May.

15 – 5 – 1962   The Customs Union is progressing: the Council decides to accelerate the process of eliminating customs duties within the Common Market.

1 – 11 – 1962   The European Economic Community and Greece sign an association agreement. The object is to promote economic rapprochement between Greece and the Community with a view to subsequent Greek accession.

Two steps forward,
one step back
1963 – 1965

14 – 1 – 1963 The first round of negotiations for Community enlargement break down. At a press conference on 14 January 1963, General de Gaulle, President of the French Republic, states that France doubts the political will of the United Kingdom to join the Community. A few days later, on 18 January, negotiations with all the applicant countries – Denmark, Ireland, Norway and the United Kingdom – are suspended.

22 – 1 – 1963 France and the Federal Republic of Germany sign a treaty of friendship and cooperation on 22 January 1963. The aim is to tighten links between the two countries and give a new impetus to the process of European integration.

11 – 7 – 1963 The unilateral halting of negotiations for Community enlargement and the signing immediately afterwards of a Franco-German Treaty of friendship have left a bitter taste in the mouths of certain Member States. Attempts are made in diplomatic circles to break out of the deadlock.

On 11 July 1963 the EEC Council proposes regular contacts with the United Kingdom via the Western European Union (WEU).

20 – 7 – 1963 Meanwhile the Community is still pursuing the negotiations commenced with the African countries late in 1961, and on 20 July 1963 the broadest association agreement ever entered into by Europe and Africa is signed at Yaoundé: the Yaoundé Convention, valid for five years, unites the Community with seventeen African States – Burundi, Cameroon, the Central African Republic, Chad, Congo Kinshasa (now called Zaïre), Congo Brazzaville, Dahomey (now called Benin), Gabon, Ivory Coast, Mali, Mauritania, Niger, Rwanda, Senegal, Somalia, Togo and Upper Volta – and Madagascar.

The Community's eighteen partners are to enjoy commercial, technical and financial cooperation on an equal footing and the agreement is scheduled to go into operation on 1 June 1964.

12 – 9 – 1963   The association agreement with Turkey is signed. Like the 1962 agreement with Greece its aim is to produce economic rapprochement with a view to ultimate Turkish accession to the European Community.

29 – 9 – 1963   Encouraged by the signing of the Yaoundé Convention, three East African countries – Kenya, Uganda, and Tanganyika (now called Tanzania) – belonging to an African common market ask for negotiations with the Community.

14 – 10 – 1963   The Community signs its first trade agreement with a non-member country – Iran.

4 – 5 – 1964   The GATT multilateral trade negotiations begin on 4 May 1964 with the Community taking part. These negotiations, which go under the name of the Kennedy Round, result in a substantial cut in international customs duties. The Community's external tariff is reduced by between 35 % and 40 % depending on the product (excepting agricultural products) and is lower than the tariffs of its major trading partners.

1 – 7 – 1964   Internally, the most important event at this time is the establishment of the common agricultural market. Market organizations are set up for most agricultural products. Uniform prices, valid only with effect from 1967, are adopted for cereals on 15 December 1964. The European Agricultural Guidance and Guarantee Fund (EAGGF) begins operating on 1 July 1964.

As most agricultural products are gradually brought under common market organizations, the Community has to solve the problem of financing the common agricultural policy.

The financial regulations in force since the beginning of 1962 are due to expire on 1 July 1965. To replace them the Commission, still with Walter Hallstein as its President, devises a bold new solution which it presents to the Council on 31 March 1965.

The plan is to give the Community its own resources by allocating to it the levies charged at the Community's frontiers on imports from non-member countries. These new resources – the Community's own resources – would be subject to review by the European Parliament, which would thus acquire major budgetary powers.

The Commission's objectives are ambitious – providing the Community with its own resources, making it financially autonomous and at the same time strengthening the powers of the European Parliament – and the Commission counts on the massive support of Parliament and of the agricultural organizations to get its plan adopted.

30 – 6 – 1965 The French Government's reaction is keenly hostile. On 30 June 1965 the Council meets in Brussels, with the French Foreign Minister, Mr Couve de Murville, in the chair.

Tension is high. Shortly after midnight, in a strained atmosphere, Mr Couve de Murville declares that no agreement has been reached within the appointed time and closes the meeting.

The next day the French Government issues a statement declaring that the Community is in a state of crisis.

And crisis there is. Not only because of the serious and unprecedented events of the night of 30 June but also because for the next seven months France operates an, 'empty chair' policy in the Community. No French representatives attend Community meetings and France's Permanent Representative to the Community in Brussels is recalled to Paris.

At the end of October the other five members issue an official Council statement calling on France to resume its place in the institutions.

1965

A compromise settlement and new beginnings 1966 – 1968

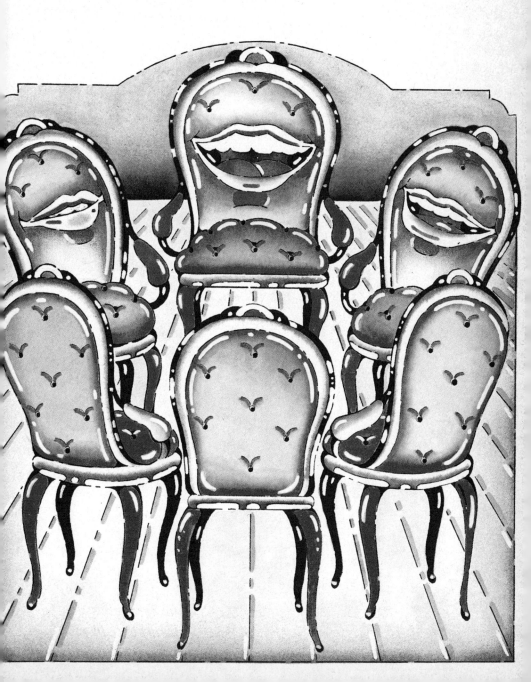

28/29 – 1 – 1966 The 1965 crisis is solved by the Luxembourg compromise: whenever one or other of the members considers that it has 'vital interests' at stake, the Council will endeavour to reach solutions acceptable to all within a reasonable time. But the six Member States nevertheless 'note that there is a divergence of views on what should be done in the event of failure to reach complete agreement'.

The result is the preservation of the unanimity rule in the Council, wrapped up in a rather tortuous formula that barely conceals the differences of opinion between the Six. From January 1966 the unanimity rule should have given way to majority voting on many of the decisions to be taken by the Council.

Following the Luxembourg compromise France resumes its place in the Community institutions.

30 – 6 – 1967 The GATT multinational trade negotiations (Kennedy Round) that opened on 4 May 1964 culminate on 30 June 1967 in a general reduction in customs tariffs by all the world's major trading countries and in new conditions for developing trade in agricultural products.

For the Community, the agreements are signed by the Member States and by the Commission.

21 – 4 – 1967 The Community puts its association with Greece on ice following the Colonels' *coup d'État*. The Colonels have abolished the Greek constitution, repealed many of the country's democratic laws and curtailed individual freedom. By freezing the association the European Community seeks to show its profound disapproval.

11 – 5 – 1967 The United Kingdom re-applies to join the Community. It is followed by Ireland and Denmark and, a little later, by Norway.

But General de Gaulle, President of the French Republic, is still reluctant to accept British accession. In view of France's refusal to commence negotiations, all the Community can do is leave the applications on its agenda.

On 1 July 1967 the Treaty signed on 8 April 1965 creating a single Council and a single Commission enters into force.

This is what is now commonly known as the merger of the executives. There is now only one Commission (replacing the

1967

ECSC High Authority and the EEC and Euratom Commissions) and one Council. But the new Commission and the Council will naturally continue to act in accordance with the rules governing each of the Communities (laid down by the three Treaties).

Consolidation
1968 – 1970

1 – 7 – 1968   The customs union is completed on 1 July 1968. Eighteen months ahead of the timetable in the EEC Treaty, all customs duties are removed in trade between Member States. At the same time the Community finally sets up its common external tariff.

18 – 12 – 1968   Sicco Mansholt, Vice-President of the Commission with particular responsibility for the common agricultural policy, launches what has come to be known as the Mansholt plan for modernization of the Community's farming sector.

Pricing policy and market organizations have not settled all the problems. There are more than 10 million persons working in agriculture. There are substantial differences in the size of farms, the number of persons working on them and the number of machines per hectare. The same applies to incomes and working conditions.

In Sicco Mansholt's memorandum the Commission describes the current situation of agriculture in Europe and points out the need for substantial structural reform. Only large, modern, rational farms can survive, the Commission argues. Yet most farms in the Community are far from satisfying the minimum structural requirements, according to the memorandum. Accordingly, the proposal advocates an active social and structural policy and a package of social measures in favour of farmers who retire or leave the land to take up some other occupation.

1/2 – 12 – 1969 The Heads of State or of Government meet at the Hague on 1 and 2 December 1969, aware that if they are to preserve the Community's achievements – and nobody wishes to destroy them – they must launch out once again with new initiatives for integration in Europe.

Following a particularly difficult period in the Community's life, the Hague summit constitutes an important step forward.

In accordance with the Treaty the Heads of State or of Government declare that the Treaty of Rome is now in the definitive stage; they call for the establishment of economic and monetary union; they speak out in favour of strengthening the Community institutions; they support the idea of enlarging the Community; and they give a new impulse to political cooperation.

They also agree on the financing of the common agricultural policy, on the creation of Community own resources and on increases in the Parliament's budgetary powers, issues which had all given rise to considerable tension before and were indeed at the origin of the empty chair crisis of June 1965.

The summit conference at the Hague thus satisfies all the great hopes that were placed in it. The Hague spirit is the symbol of a political will that the Member States have rediscovered. Its resolutions make for the consolidation, strengthening and enlargement of the Community.

9 – 2 – 1970   The governors of the central banks sign an agreement setting up a short-term monetary support system. This is a practical step towards greater monetary solidarity between the Community Member States.

21/22 – 4 – 1970 Decisions are quickly taken on the Community's own resources. Under the new system the Community will receive all customs duties on products imported from non-member

1970

countries and all levies on agricultural imports, together with up to 1 % of value added tax (VAT) levied on a uniform basis within the Member States. The Parliaments of the Member States rapidly ratify these arrangements, which provide the Community with the beginnings of a real financial autonomy.

27 – 10 – 1970   On 27 October 1970 the Member States approve the Davignon report on political cooperation, a direct sequel of the Hague summit.

With this report the Member States adopt the principle of periodic meetings of Foreign Ministers and heads of Foreign Ministry political departments. The idea is to concert and if possible harmonize Member States' policies and viewpoints in the foreign affairs field.

The objectives set out in the report, often known as the Luxembourg report after the place where it was adopted, are: regular exchanges of information and consultations so as to improve mutual understanding on the great international problems of the day; greater solidarity between the Member States by promoting harmonization of their views, by coordinating their positions and by undertaking joint actions wherever this is possible and desirable.

The new objective that the Member States have assigned themselves is to get Europe to speak with a single voice on all major international and world problems and to act together wherever it can and wherever it must.

Enlargement
and monetary problems
1970 – 1973

Community enlargement and the attainment of economic and monetary union are the top priorities between 1970 and 1972.

30 – 6 – 1970

22 – 1— 1972

New negotiations for the accession of Denmark, Ireland, Norway and the United Kingdom begin on 30 June 1970. They are difficult negotiations as they extend to virtually every area of economic and political life. On 22 January 1972 the Treaties of Accession are signed. They are rapidly ratified by the Parliaments of the old Member States and of the new Member States except Norway, where a referendum is held and the Accession Treaty is rejected by a narrow majority (53 %).

The new Community of Nine dates from 1 January 1973.

7 – 10 – 1970

The Hague summit has given the impulse for the creation of an economic and monetary union. It has been found that the pursuit of European integration means there have to be common or at least coordinated economic policies. In October 1970 a committee of financial and monetary experts chaired by Luxembourg Prime Minister Pierre Werner presents the governments with a plan for the progressive unification of economic policies and the creation of a monetary organization designed to culminate by 1980 in the attainment of full economic and monetary union with a common currency.

The measures to be taken for the achievement of this ambitious objective concern economic, monetary and budgetary policy, capital movements and tax and income policies.

22 – 3 – 1971

The Council decides that the first stage of the Werner Plan will have retroactive effect from 1 January 1971 and proceeds to strengthen the coordination of economic policies. The Member States are to take measures to harmonize their budgetary policies and to reduce the margins of fluctuation between their currencies.

But the launching of the economic and monetary union is immediately disrupted by the monetary crisis of 1971. The Community is not responsible for the crisis but bears much of the brunt. The crisis arises from the overvaluation of the US dollar against gold and currencies valued in terms of gold.

In August 1971 the US Government suspends convertibility of the dollar into gold, thereby jeopardizing the whole Bretton Woods monetary system and the parity equilibrium of most Western currencies.

Right in the middle of the summer holiday period, governments, banks and the Community authorities consider the situation and take steps to deal with the immediate problems.

Exchange rates between the currencies of the Member States continue to diverge wildly under the pressures of the market.

Only in December 1971 are the monetary authorities able to restore a degree of order. What happens basically is that the US dollar and the Italian lira are devalued, the Deutschmark, the Dutch guilder, the Belgian franc, the Japanese yen and the Swiss franc are revalued and the French franc and sterling maintain their old gold parities.

In April 1972 the Six decide that the maximum margins for fluctuation of their exchange rates must be brought back to 2.25 %. Although the United Kingdom, Ireland and Denmark are not to become full Community members until January 1973, they nevertheless join the new system, baptised the snake.

But despite this decision, which creates an important link between the currencies of the Member States and consequently between their economic and monetary policies, there can be no escaping the fact that the march towards economic and monetary union now has to begin again.

The dollar crisis is the apparent cause of the failure of the plan for the first stage of economic and monetary union, which has been in operation since 1 January 1971. But the real reasons for the failure are deeper rooted. They lie in the differing structures and policies of the Member States and in their varying capacity to resist external pressure.

While the health of the dollar is quickly restored, the European currencies are still tottering. Sterling, the Irish pound and the French franc are unable to remain within the maximum margin of fluctuation in relation to the currencies of the other Community countries. Sterling and the Irish pound are withdrawn from the snake in June 1972 and the French franc in February 1973.

21/22 – 6 – 1971 The Community offers the non-associated developing countries the benefit of the generalized preferences scheme, under which all developing countries that enjoy no special relations with the Community are given more advantageous customs tariff treatment than is applied to rich countries.

1971

19/20 – 10 –
1972

The Heads of State or of Government meet at a summit conference in Paris to define new fields of Community action – regional policy, environment policy and energy policy – not provided for by the Treaties. They reaffirm the 1980 deadline for the attainment of economic and monetary union.

The energy crisis,
beginning of the economic crisis
1973 – 1974

1 – 1 – 1973   Enlargement of the European Community takes effect on 1 January 1973. Economically and commercially the Community of Nine is a power to be reckoned with on the world scene. There are still those that regard it as a political dwarf, but it is nevertheless gaining in credibility. Much depends politically on the ability of the Nine to speak with a single voice when offering views or acting on the international stage.

The United States invites the enlarged Community to new multilateral trade negotiations within GATT. These begin in Tokyo in September 1973.

The Soviet Union, originally hostile to the Community, begins to take a more realistic view of things and recognizes realities in Europe.

The Community's activities in relation to the Third World are expanding considerably. The Community continues and extends its agreements with the associated States. In July 1973 negotiations begin not only with the Yaoundé Convention countries, which since 1972 include Mauritius, but also with twenty-seven other developing countries in Africa, the Caribbean and the Pacific (ACP), twenty-four of them Commonwealth countries. The main object is to broaden the Yaoundé Convention following Community enlargement, to take in countries that have special relations with the United Kingdom and a few other countries. The new convention will concern developing countries with an aggregate population of 240 million.

1 – 1 – 1973   On 1 January 1973 free-trade agreements come into force between the Community and some of the EFTA countries that have not joined the Community. These countries are Austria, Portugal, Switzerland and Sweden. Agreements with the other EFTA members, Iceland, Norway and Finland, come into force later. As a result of the agreements the common external tariff does not apply between these countries and the Community. The EFTA countries thus enjoy a customs union with the Community but do not participate in the Communities' common policies.

October 1973   The Yom Kippur war between Israel and Egypt provokes the Arab countries into decreeing an embargo on petroleum exports to the Netherlands and a substantial reduction in supplies to other industrial countries; but, worse still, the petroleum exporting countries belonging to OPEC quadruple the price of crude oil.

The Community, which imports 63 % of its energy requirements, mostly in the form of petroleum from the Middle East, is hard hit.

The fourfold rise in the price of petroleum has a direct economic impact – it forces up the cost of manufactured products and throws balances of payment into disequilibrium.

Unfortunately, despite the Commission's efforts, the 1973 energy crisis does not have the advantage of inspiring a common energy policy.

5 – 11 – 1973 In November 1973 the Member States, at a political cooperation meeting, put out a joint statement on the situation in the Middle East and on the conditions for a peaceful settlement of the conflict.

14/15 – 12 – 1973 But at the summit conference in Copenhagen they fail to agree on a common response to the increase in oil prices, though at least they agree – not for the first time – on the need for rapid development of a common energy policy.

April 1974 In the United Kingdom the Labour Party, having promised the voters that it would renegotiate the terms of accession, wins the elections, replaces the Conservative Party in government and, in April 1974, seeks renegotiation of the accession terms.

Once again the Community embarks on a difficult period. The European Council at Dublin in March 1975 produces a solution to the problem of the British contribution to the Community budget. The British barrier to progress is lifted in June 1975 when the British people, consulted at a referendum, votes by a large majority to stay in the European Community.

9/10 – 12 – 1974 The purpose of the December 1974 summit meetings of Heads of State or of Government in Paris is to relax the tension in the Community, release the Community from a number of its internal problems and enable it to get on with its real work.

Community leaders meet against a background of the energy crisis, the economic difficulties which this crisis has aggravated, the monetary chaos of 1973 – 1974, Britain's request to renegotiate the terms of accession, and the inability of the Community to move on to the second stage of economic and monetary union at the beginning of 1974 as planned.

At the Paris summit agreement is reached on the resources to be allocated by the Community to the European Regional Development Fund (ERDF) from 1975 onwards.

1974

The Heads of State or of Government accept the suggestion from the chair that they should meet three times a year and whenever necessary as the European Council, to debate not only European affairs but also important questions of foreign policy.

The European Council is born, to supersede the earlier summit meetings held at less regular intervals.

But the most important decision taken at Paris by the Heads of State or of Government concerns the election of the European Parliament by direct universal suffrage.

The Belgian Prime Minister, Mr Leo Tindemans, is instructed to prepare a report on how to transform the Community into a European union embracing the whole complex of relations between the Member States, as envisaged at the 1972 summit.

Further enlargement and direct elections 1975 – 1979

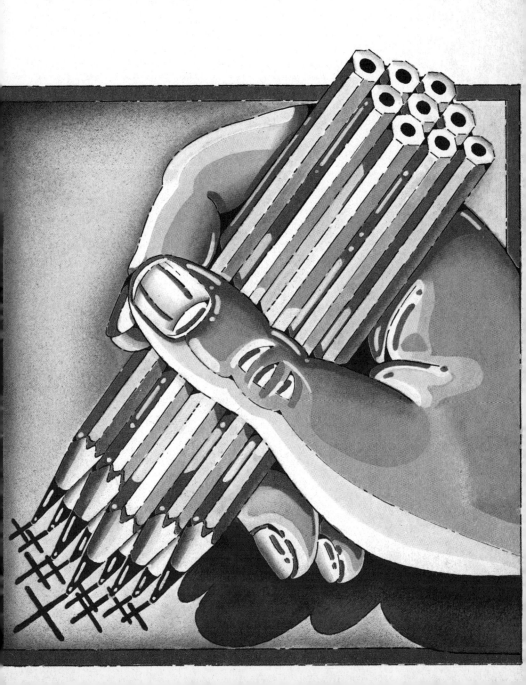

1975	In 1975 and the years that follow, unemployment re-emerges as a major problem in all the Member States, economies slow down and the difficulties besetting several industries – especially textiles, shipbuilding and steel – grow steadily worse.
28 – 2 – 1975	The European Community and forty-six countries of Africa, the Caribbean and the Pacific (ACP) sign the Lomé Convention to replace both the 1963 and 1969 Yaoundé Conventions (bringing together the Community and eighteen African countries plus Madagascar) and the Arusha Agreement. The Lomé Convention provides for commercial cooperation and gives virtually all products originating in the ACP countries free access to the Community market; it guarantees the ACP countries stable export earnings from thirty-six commodities, thus shielding them against fluctuations in world market prices; it provides for industrial and financial cooperation; and, like the two earlier conventions, it operates through joint institutions in which all the parties have their say in the management of the agreements.
16 – 2 – 1976	There are contacts with Comecon which is seeking outline agreements with the Community. Negotiations have not yet been concluded.
April 1976 January 1977	The Community enters into agreements with the Maghreb countries (Tunisia, Algeria and Morocco) in April 1976 and with the Mashreq countries (Egypt, Syria, Jordan and Lebanon) in January 1977. By these agreements and the agreement made with Israel on 11 May 1975, the Commission implements its global Mediterranean policy.

The agreements with these southern Mediterranean countries provide for the removal or reduction of customs duties on

most of the products that the Community imports from them; they also provide for economic, technical and financial cooperation. As regards the Maghreb countries, which have 800 000 of their citizens working in the Community, the agreements guarantee the same working conditions and social security rights as are enjoyed by nationals of Community countries.

12 – 6 – 1975
28 – 3 – 1977
28 – 7 – 1977 Applications for accession to the Community are received from Greece (12 June 1975), Portugal (28 March 1977) and Spain (28 July 1977). These countries, all of which have recently returned to the democratic fold, would extend the Community southwards and add 9 million Greeks, 9 million Portuguese and 35 million Spaniards to its population.

The second enlargement will raise a series of new problems for the Community because of the differences between levels of development in the applicant countries and in the Community.

On the other hand enlargement will confirm the political basis for the integration of Europe and will strengthen the Community's position in the world.

Solutions will have to be found to the problems of the institutional operations of a Community of twelve Member States.

1 – 12 – 1975 In Rome the European Council finally decides on the election of the European Parliament by direct universal suffrage, the principle having been adopted at the Paris summit. It decides that the first elections will take place in spring 1978, but this is later postponed to 7 to 10 June 1979.

A directly-elected Parliament was called for by the Treaties. It has taken the Community twenty-five years to reach agreement on it.

The new Parliament is to have 410 members (there were 198 in the old Parliament) – 81 each from France, Germany, Italy and the United Kingdom, 25 from the Netherlands, 24 from Belgium, 16 from Denmark, 15 from Ireland and 6 from Luxembourg.

29 – 12 – 1975 Mr Leo Tindemans, the Belgian Prime Minister, presents the governments of the Member States with his report on European Union, called for at the Paris summit. In preparing it Mr Tindemans has had consultations with all the Community institutions, the governments of all the Member States, and a broad spectrum of political parties, business associations and trade unions.

In order gradually to fuse the relations of the Member States into a European Union, Mr Tindemans proposes a series of measures including a common external policy, an economic and monetary union, European social and regional policies, joint industrial policies as regards growth industries, policies directly affecting Community citizens and a substantial reinforcement of the Community institutions.

The Tindemans Report has regularly been on the European Council's agenda, but no direct action has yet been taken on it.

April 1978 The Community signs a trade agreement with China, with which it established relations in 1975.

Even before then China had always insisted on the need for a strong, united Europe.

The trade agreement with the world's most populous country, which was so long kept off the international political scene, is greeted optimistically by the Member States.

April – The European Councils in April (Copenhagen), July (Bre-
December 1978 men) and December (Brussels) are largely devoted to seeking ways out of the problems created for the Community by the persistence of the economic difficulties and to the establishment of a European Monetary System (EMS).

9/10 – 3 – 1979 The European Council at Paris brings the EMS into operation. The decision had already been taken in Brussels in December before, but had been held up pending agreement on monetary problems in the agricultural sector.

The EMS has four main components – a European currency unit (ECU), an exchange and information mechanism, credit facilities and transfer arrangements.

The European currency unit is the heart of the system.

Initially the United Kingdom prefers not to play a full part in the EMS.

The operation of the EMS will have to be accompanied by greater convergence of economic policies. Measures are also planned to boost the economic potential of the less prosperous Community countries.

1979

28 – 5 – 1979   In Athens, Greece and the Community sign the Treaty of Accession; Greece will become the tenth Member State of the Community with effect from 1 January 1981. The Treaty has to be ratified by the Parliaments of the Member States and of Greece.

The Greek Government applied for membership on 12 June 1975, and negotiations officially opened in July 1976.

With Greek accession to the European Community, southward enlargement begins. Negotiations with Portugal and Spain are continuing.

Greek accession will take place over a five-year transitional period during which the Greek economy will gradually adapt to the higher economic level of the Community, which will give it substantial financial assistance for the purpose. The addition of 9.2 million Greeks will raise the Community's population to 269 million.

But over and above the purely economic implications, enlargement this time will have the profoundest historical and cultural significance, for Greece is the birthplace of European civilization and democracy.

7/10 – 6 – 1979   In the first direct election the citizens of the nine Member States vote for the 410 members of the European Parliament.

The overall turnout is 61 %. The figures for the individual countries are as follows: Belgium 91.4 %, Luxembourg 85 % (voting is compulsory in these two countries), Italy 85.5 %, Federal Republic of Germany 65.9 %, Ireland 63.6 %, France 61.3 %, Netherlands 57.8 %, Denmark 47 % (Greenland 33 %), United Kingdom 32.6 %.

This historic election, which is conducted in each country on the basis of the national electoral system, produces the following groups in the Parliament: Socialists 112 members, European People's Party (Christian-Democrats) 108 members, European Democratic Group 64 members, Communists 44 members, Liberal and Democratic Group 39 members, European Progressive Democrats 22 members, Group for the Technical Coordination and Defence of Independent Groups and Members 11 members, and the remaining 10 members non-attached.

The directly-elected Parliament holds its first sitting on 17 July. In a second ballot the House elects as its first President Mrs Simone Veil, the former Minister of Health and Family Affairs in the French Government.

Main agreements between the European Community and the rest of the world

The list below sets out the main agreements between the Community and the rest of the world on which it was impossible to comment in detail in this booklet.

It can be seen that the Community has agreements with most of the world's countries.

Multilateral agreements

General agreements for the mutual reduction of tariff barriers within GATT and connected arrangements:

> **Dillon Round (1960 – 1962)**
> **Kennedy Round (1963 – 1967)**
> **Tokyo Round (under negotiation)**
> **Anti-Dumping Code (1967)**

Commodity agreements, with the chief objective of stabilizing markets:

> **International Grains Arrangement (GATT 1967)**
> **International Skimmed-Milk Powder Arrangement (GATT 1970)**
> **Long-Term Arrangement regarding International Trade in Cotton Textiles (GATT 1970)**
> **Multifibre Arrangement (GATT 1973, renewed 1978)**
> **International Tin Agreement (UNCTAD 1970, 1976)**
> **International Wheat Agreement (1971)**
> **International Coffee Agreement (1976)**
> **International Cocoa Agreement (1976)**

Association agreements combining various instruments of commercial, industrial, financial and technical cooperation:

> **EEC/East Africa Association:**
> **Arusha Agreement (1968/1969)**
> **ECC/AASM Association: Yaoundé Conventions (1963/1969)**
> **EEC/ACP Association: Lomé Convention (1975)**

Bilateral agreements

Association agreements intended to lead ultimately to accession to the Community:

Greece (1961), Turkey (1963)

Free-trade agreements confined to industrial products and involving consultation procedures (joint committees):

Austria (1973), Switzerland (1973), Portugal (1973), Sweden (1973), Iceland (1973), Norway (1973) and Finland (1974)

Agreements forming part of the overall approach to the Mediterranean, offering the Community's partners free access to its market for industrial products and concessionary terms for imports of agricultural produce, coupled with financial assistance and consultation procedures:

Israel (1975), Algeria (1976), Tunisia (1976), Morocco (1976), Malta (1976), Egypt (1977), Jordan (1977), Syria (1977), Lebanon (1977) and Cyprus (1978)

Outline agreement for economic and commercial cooperation designed as an instrument for developing cooperation in the full range of activities, both at government and at business level. Institutionalization of a joint cooperation committee:

Canada (1976)

Preferential agreement for the gradual removal of barriers to trade in most products:

Spain (1970)

Commercial cooperation agreements with the object of promoting development and diversification of trade. Joint committees to devise the most suitable measures for the purpose:

India (1973), Sri Lanka (1975), Mexico (1975), Pakistan (1976), Bangladesh (1976) and China (1978)

Trade agreements designed principally to facilitate imports of specified products in the Community:

Iran (1963), Yugoslavia (1973), Argentina (1971), Uruguay (1973) and Brazil (1973)

Agreements with specific subject matters:

Textiles, fibres, steel, certain handicraft products, cooperation on the peaceful uses of nuclear energy, fisheries, Euratom-United States Agreement, agreement guaranteeing Indian sugar exports.

Further reading

Matthews, Jacqueline D.
Association system of the European Community.
New York (etc.): Praeger 1977. XVII, 167 pp. Bibliogr. pp. 156 – 163.

Sjoestedt, Gunnar
(The) external role of the European Community. Swedish Institute of International Affairs, Stockholm.
Westmead: Saxon House 1977. VIII, 273 pp. Bibliogr. pp. 265 – 270.
= Swedish studies in international relations 7

Edwards, Geoffrey; Wallace, William
(A) wider European Community? Issues and problems of further enlargement. London: The Federal Trust for Education and Research 1976.

Paxton, John
The developing Common Market. 3rd ed.
London: Macmillan 1976. 240 pp.

Mowat, R. C.
Creating the European Community.
London: Blandford 1973. 235 pp. Bibliogr. pp. 223 – 226.

Pryce, Roy
The politics of the European Community.
London: Butterworth 1973. X, 209 pp. Bibliogr. pp. 198 – 201.
= European Community Studies.

The European Community in the 1970s. Ed. by Steven Joshua Warnecke.
Publ. for the European Studies Committee. Graduate Division, City University of New York.
New York: Praeger 1972. XXII, 228 pp.
= Praeger special studies in international politics and public affairs.

Morgan, Roger
West European politics since 1945. The shaping of the European Community.
London: Batsford 1972. 243 pp.

Mayne, Richard
The recovery of Europe. From devastation to Unity.
London: Weidenfeld and Nicolson 1970. 374 pp. Bibliogr. pp. 335 – 358.

Lindberg, Leon N.; Scheingold, Stuart A.
Europe's would-be policy. Patterns of change in the European Community.
Book written under the auspices of the Center for International Affairs, Harvard Univ.
Englewood Cliffs, N. J.: Prentice-Hall 1970. VI, 314 pp.

The political development of the European Community. A documentary collection.
Ed. by Howard Bliss.
Waltham: Blaisdell Publ. 1970. XII, 316 pp. Bibliogr. pp. 314 – 316.
= Blaisdell book in political science.

Haas, Ernst B.
The Uniting of Europe. Political, social and economic forces.
1950 – 1957. Reissued with a new preface.
Stanford, Cal.: Stanford Univ. pr. 1968. XL, 552 pp.

Silj, Alessandro
Europe's political puzzle. A study of the Fouchet negotiations and the 1963 veto.
Cambridge (Mass.): Center for International Affairs, Harvard Univ. 1967. V, 178 pp.
= Occasional papers in international affairs. No 17.

Lister, Louis
Europe's Coal and Steel Community. An experiment in economic union.
New York: The Twentieth Century Fund 1960. 495 pp.

Diebold, William
The Schuman Plan. A study in economic cooperation 1950 – 1959. Published for the
Council on Foreign Relations.
New York: Praeger 1959. XVIII, 750 pp.

Zurcher, Arnold J.
The struggle to unite Europe 1940 – 1958. An historical account of the development of
the contemporary European movement from its origin in the Pan-European Union to
the drafting of the treaties for Euratom and the European Common Market.
New York: University Press 1958. XIX, 254 pp.

EUROPEAN COMMUNITIES – INFORMATION

Commission of the European Communities, Rue de la Loi 200, B-1049 Bruxelles.

Information offices

DUBLIN: 29 Merrion Square,
Dublin 2,
tel. 76 0353.

LONDON: 20 Kensington Palace Gardens,
London W8 4QQ,
tel. 727 8090.

BELFAST: 9/15 Bedford Street,
Windsor House.

CARDIFF: 4 Cathedral Road,
Cardiff CFI 9SG,
tel. 27 1631.

EDINBURGH: 7 Alva Street,
Edinburgh EH2 4PH.
tel. 225 2058.

OTTAWA: Inn of the Provinces – Office Tower
(Suite 1110), 350 Sparks Street,
Ottawa, Ont. KIR 7S8,
tel. 238 6464.

WASHINGTON: 2100 M. Street, N. W.
(Suite 707), Washington, DC 20037-USA,
tel. 202 862 9500.

NEW YORK: 1 Dag Hammarskjöld Plaza.
245 East 47th Street,
New York, NY 10017-USA,
tel. 212 371 3804.

Sales offices

IRELAND: Government Publications,
Sales Office, G.P.O. Arcade,
Dublin 1.

Stationery Office,
Dublin 4,
tel. 78 9644.

UNITED KINGDOM: H. M. Stationery Office,
P.O. Box 569, London SE1 9NH,
tel. 928 6977, ext. 365.

GRAND DUCHY OF LUXEMBOURG:
Office for Official Publications
of the European Communities,
Boîte postale 1003, Luxembourg,
tel. 49 00 81.

**For more information
about the European Community:**

Authors' service:

Division IX D 11 'Coordination and preparation of publications'

European Communities – Commission

Steps to European unity
Community progress to date: a chronology

Luxembourg: Office for Official Publications of the European Communities

1980 – 67 pp., 22 ill. – 16,2 × 22.9 cm

DA, DE, EN, FR, IT, NL

ISBN 92-825-1552-4

Catalogue number: CB-28-79-641-EN-C

BFR 60	DKR 10	DM 3,50	FF 8
LIT 1 800	HFL 4	UKL 1	USD 2

This booklet describes how the European Community has developed year by year from its beginnings to 1979.

Comments are added on some of the events to make them more easily accessible to the widest possible public.

19

| BFR 60 | DKR 10 | DM 3,50 | FF 8 | LIT 1 800 | HFL 4 | UKL 1 | USD 2 |

**OFFICE FOR OFFICIAL PUBLICATIONS
OF THE EUROPEAN COMMUNITIES**

ISBN 92-825-1552-4

Boîte postale 1003 – Luxembourg

Catalogue number: CB-28-79-641-EN-C

032